Dark Cloud

Cynthia Bergen

2019

Dark Cloud

Copyright © 2019 by Cynthia Bergen

All rights reserved. This book or any portion thereof may not be reproduced or used in any manner whatsoever without the expressed written permission of the publisher.

First Printing: 2019

ISBN: 978-0-9970651-1-4

i&R Publishing
7979 Broadway #209
San Antonio, TX 78209
https://iandrpublishing.wordpress.com

Ordering Information:
Special discounts are available on quantity purchases by corporations, associations, educators, and others. For details, contact the publisher at the above listed address.

Thank you to

Editor/Graphic Designer, Ajani Abdul-Khaliq

Writer/Director, Isaac Rodriguez

Prison Historian, Jolene Blakely

Web Creator, Ryan Gernsbacher

i&R Publishing

Photography by Cynthia Bergen

Special thanks to my mother
Ruth Woods, The Eternal Light

Contents

The Courtroom	1
Road Trip	3
The Tour	9
The Cell	15
Warden	21
Contact	23
Payment	35
Pictures	37
Procedures	43
Hawk	45
The Delivery	47
The Meal	51
The Execution	53
The Arrival	57

Thou shalt love thy neighbour as thyself.

- Matthew 22:39

Thou shalt not kill.

- Exodus 20:13

The Courtroom

"Timothy Walt Thomas, by the State of Texas you have been sentenced to Death."

Timothy sat motionless. All he could think of now was that same flashback to when he held the gun to the young kid's head and pulled the trigger. With his friend next to him, a yell sounded "What the fuck!" But Timothy just glared at the kid, still moving on the floor. He shot him again then ran out. Later while lying in his bed at his grandmother's house, Timothy was suddenly awakened—startled with a gun pointed in his face as the officer sternly stated, "You are under arrest for murder."

Back in court, the family of the murdered victim gave no cheers when the verdict was announced. One lady dressed in black stood up and left the courtroom, perhaps satisfied with the verdict. Then a spokesperson for the victim's family stood up and yelled at the defendant, "How can you be so cold, my cousin Daniel was only 18 years old! He was gonna join the military in three days to serve our country for you!" Pointing his finger at Timothy, the person went on. "He only had one dollar in the register! Is that why you killed him!? You didn't even think to look in the drop box! It had a whole $500 in it and was wide open, YOU FOOL!" As he sat down, another young man stood up. "You killed my friend, and a co-worker of yours once. Don't you remember that? I'll never forget when he showed me the birthday card he was going to give to you."

With nothing more to be said, court was adjourned. Timothy was escorted out of the courtroom, handcuffed and shackled with a guard and his lawyer at his side. Before going back into his cell, Timothy was told by his lawyer, "You are going to be transported to Huntsville in the morning. I will try to go before the judge again to get another trial set up…By the way, just to let you know, your partner Samuel didn't get the death penalty, but he'll be in prison for a long time." Timothy listened but did not utter a word.

As Timothy was being escorted back to his cell, the lawyer stood there looking at the newly sentenced young man. Procedure would not allow him to go any further. Instead, the lawyer could only watch. "18 years old over a dollar." He shook his head in disgust and left.

Back in his cell, Timothy just sat there. The small space with its immovable iron bars had been his home for close to a year. Lights out. Later that night while making his rounds checking all the cells, a guard happened to turn around only to be startled by a shadowy Timothy, standing there behind the bars. "What the fuck man?" the guard jumped.

Without blinking an eye Timothy answered, "I don't want to die."

Road Trip

The next morning, shackled and handcuffed, with transfer paperwork in his hand for in processing.

Timothy was escorted into a white van that had two armed guards in the front and one in the back. But the guard in the passenger seat refused to take voyages like these too seriously. "Okay boys let's buckle up! Three hour road trip." Timothy sat still and began thinking about his childhood.

He had never known his biological dad while growing up. His mom would leave him with her parents. But when she was there, he had the greatest time with her. Until one day she never returned. He would ask his grandma and grandpa when she would be back, and they would always answer, tomorrow." The next day, like clockwork, he would wait on the front porch, only to find no sign of her. From four to seven days the waiting continued. Until one day he finally decided to stay in his room.

Timothy's school was in walking distance. So his grandpa, using a cane, would walk with him to and from school. This became a daily ritual. The Catholic school he attended was easily the most beautiful architectural structure he had ever seen. But he developed a hatred for seeing other kids there with their parents, especially the ones who were full of energy, doing things like playing sports together. Timothy would often see the other kids staring at him, laughing and saying ugly things about his grandpa—who they claimed was his biological father. Grandpa used to say, "don't pay them any attention, they don't know any better." But the teasing still bothered Timothy.

As the years went on Timothy was getting expelled from school more and more often. By the time he reached the age of 15 he was a dropout. Got a girl he was dating pregnant, and suddenly became a father at 16. Problems seemed to follow Timothy everywhere, but most of those problems came from him hanging out with the wrong people. It was no surprise then that dealing drugs became his main source of income even though he had free room and board with his grandparents. He did manage to avoid getting hooked on them himself, though. Dealing drugs and using them didn't mix with him. And life went on, struggle after struggle. Until one night Timothy returned home to find his girlfriend and his little son gone. That's when things took a turn for the worst.

Now here he was on death row. Looking out of the van and at the surroundings, he knew this would be the last trip on this road. One of the guards up front motioned to the driver, "Almost to Houston. We're gonna be fueling up, then potty breaks." As soon as they finally pulled into a gas station, the guard went inside. After a while he came back. "Okay everything is secured." They opened the side door and Timothy slowly came out in shackles.

Road Trip

Some of the customers at the gas station stopped in their tracks and watched. Timothy could only pretend he was not humiliated. As they went inside, a convenience store clerk said to one of the guards, "you make sure he doesn't get away because I have the biggest shot gun here ready to blow that motherfucker away."

The guard looked at him, "We got it under control."

As the group exited the convenience store, it seemed like word had spread. There were more people gathering outside to stare as they left. As they reentered the van, the driver told the guard in the passenger seat, "Next time let's just piss on the side of the road."

Passing through Houston. Timothy sat silently taking everything in, squinting through the bar lined windows of the van. He had never been to Houston. Was this like a vacation? Yes! A kind of vacation to Hell. Further into East Texas Timothy took note of the pine trees. *Now it's all coming back*, he reflected. Grandpa used to take him fishing in this area when they would go visit relatives. *Nothing like the smell of pine.*

As far as Timothy understood, he was not going to be kept in Huntsville itself but somewhere on the outskirts. At least that's what his lawyer had told him. At some point along the drive, one of the guards noticed some cops up ahead. Upon closer approach everyone could see that there was a roadblock. "You got to be shitting me," the driver groaned. But the guard in the passenger seat figured his cargo had priority no matter what the situation was, so there should be no problem. Arriving even closer, however, the cops and the roadblock brought along with them another obstacle. A railroad crossing.

The guard in the passenger seat told the driver to pull over so they could find out what the problem was.

As the guard approached the railroad tracks, he noticed two yellow tarps covering some hidden contents, maybe five yards from each other. Being a police officer, he immediately guessed that the tarps were not covering plants, but bodies. The cop in charge of the scene saw the guard and called out, "Sir is that your white van up yonder?"

"Yes!" the guard answered right away.

"Well sir this is a crime scene and no one and I mean no one is allowed to pass through here," the cop warned.

"Sir we just might have a problem, then. I'm escorting a prisoner on death row and they are expecting him to arrive in—" The guard glanced at his watch. "—in one hour."

The crime scene cop was unimpressed. "As you know being an officer yourself you cannot and I mean CANNOT go through this crime scene!" The guard knew this was a no go, but it left him time to do a little investigating himself.

"So may I ask what happened since I can't go through? I see you have two bodies covered."

The officer replied, "Let me correct you. It's only one body. Cut in half by the train."

Road Trip

And with that comment, the guard turned around and walked back to the van.

As he got back inside the vehicle, the guard immediately told the driver to turn around.

"What!?" the driver protested.

"We'll have to go the long route. Which will take us through Huntsville."

The driver's look turned to panic. "You know I hate going through that! that! place!" But the passenger seat guard just looked at him. The driver turned the van around.

The Tour

Timothy sat in the back taking in the sights, knowing this would be the last time. The guard in the passenger seat sensed at this point that the driver was a pussy. So, knowing Huntsville like the back of his hand, the passenger seat guard decided to have some fun.

"Turn here," the guard motioned to the driver. Before long, they approached a sign reading, "Welcome to Huntsville." The guard glanced over at the driver, who had clearly tensed up. With a smirk on his face, he thought to himself, *This is going to be so much fun*, even if they *did* have a murderer in the back.

While driving on the highway, the group spotted a tall white image emerging in the distance. As they got closer, the guard in the passenger seat decided to act as tour guide. Timothy with his head down, slowly lifted it up. To him this was just what he needed. A distraction. The guard began explaining the white figure they were approaching.

"Look up ahead. As you can see, the closer we come the bigger it gets."

Dark Cloud

The driver grumbled immediately, "Bob can you please—we're escorting a prisoner not a vacationer."

"*This* is the statue of Sam Houston, and if you look just beyond the trees there's a statue of his head." The guard in the passenger seat kept on talking as though there were no driver at all. "Why the head? I don't know."

The guard turned a goofy quiz show host's eyebrow at the driver. "Okay Ken, how much did you learn?"

Ken the driver stared straight ahead, annoyed. He didn't say a word.

Timothy decided to keep his head up and look at all of the surroundings. He saw one house they passed that looked like a shack, but then again wasn't. It had one big cross in the middle and two small crosses on the side. There was something odd about this. What kind of worship went on there? Then another one. Later, another. It seemed like there was a church or two on every block. While his eyes were busy following the rolling backdrop, Timothy happened to look up front. Through the rear-view mirror, Ken the driver was staring at him with hate.

The Tour

The Three Crosses

As they entered the downtown section, Bob the guard resumed his tour guiding. "Do you know this town has a total of 20 prisons?" He motioned to the driver, "Ken, make a turn here. This is Sam Houston State University. At this college they have one of the largest body harvesting farms for science. Where do you think they get most of their bodies from?"

(Silence.)

Timothy's stare remained fixed on an old car that had been traveling next to them for a while. Behind the wheel of the car sat a very old black man with a tired hat crookedly flopped on his head, and what looked like a cigar hanging out of his mouth. One more thing, the old man never turned his head. *Odd.* Again, Timothy looked up at the rear-view mirror. Ken the driver was still staring at him. *Doesn't he ever—*

"Watch Out!" Bob suddenly yelled. Ken swerved to avoid that very car with the old man. A single hard slam on the brakes sent both Timothy and the third guard in the back falling out of their seats. As the van came to an abrupt stop, the guard in the back picked himself up. Then he helped Timothy back into his seat. The old man had tried merging at a stop light turned red and just kept on going.

Ken shouted like an angry baby, "Get that motherfucker out of this van!" He pointed an extra-accusatory finger at Timothy. "We need to get the fuck out of this town!"

Bob just stared at Ken again. No words at all. He did, however, motion to make a right.

A Dangerous Driver

Glancing to the right, Bob noted that they were now passing a red brick building called "The Walls Unit." This was where they did the executions.

Minutes later, the white van crossed a bridge that stretched over a huge lake. Timothy still couldn't get over the old man in the car. There wasn't much time to think about it though. In

The Tour

no time they approached a building with an armed guard posted at the front gate. Timothy knew they were at the destination.

Bob handed Ken some paperwork to hand to the gate guard in turn. The armed guard looked inside the van and signaled for them to proceed. Timothy's palms sweat heavily as the building's walls covered him in their shade. This would be his next home and his last glimpse of freedom. Once they had parked, Bob got out of the van and went inside the building. Seconds later he came out and motioned to the guard in the back seat to open up. Timothy was escorted from the van, and led through the gates and some high heavy metal doors that slammed very loudly.

Hearing his footsteps echo down the corridor as he hobbled to keep up, Timothy wished they could execute him right there. Why wait five or ten years?

At the front desk stood three guards and a man dressed in a suit. While Bob waited for the initial in-processing to clear, the gentleman in the suit approached and greeted the new prisoner. "Well Welcome to our humble home…" He looked down at the paperwork, "…Timothy."

"I am not going to give you a long lecture. All I can tell you is, just keep your nose clean. Good behavior is a wonderful thing around here." The man in the suit turned around, "Right gentlemen? The guards nodded their heads, then one of them stepped forward.

Dark Cloud

"Okay we will take it from here."

Bob guided Timothy through the gate as the van escort exchanged shackles and handcuffs with the prison guards. Bob's job was done, inmate delivered. Timothy jumped when the row of bars on the run slammed closed.

As soon as Bob arrived back at the van, he looked at Ken, "What. Is. Your. Fucking problem, man!?" To which Ken answered with a mixture of irritation and fear.

Ken's voice shook a little. "This place, this town, is fucking haunted. Look at the sun! It's only 5:00 in the afternoon! Look at the clouds man. They're dark. This shit is not normal." And that prisoner we had. We had three things happen to us. You know things come in threes."

The Cell

Timothy finally made it to his cell after in-processing (which seemed like another word for being probed in every crevice possible on a human body). *Gone through it before, but look on the bright side. This is the last time.* But who could know what new troubles awaited? Slowly looking around his room, he saw it as the same old shit but a little larger. *Wow, moving on up!* Sitting contemplating after a few seconds, Timothy considered what to do. *Should I sit up and think or lie down? Don't know, but I *do not* want to fall asleep.*

A loud voice plowed through Timothy's ears, shaking him back into the waking world. "5020!" Opening his eyes, Timothy saw the shadow of a person standing there. Slowly, reality set in and he realized it was a prison guard. "Just for that 5020 you are coming with me!" The guard ordered Timothy to turn around. That is when the darkness followed.

Awakening as he attempted to gather his focus, Timothy tried to rub his forehead but couldn't. He tried to move his hands but couldn't. He looked down. They were both strapped. That's when Timothy panicked! *What the Fuck!*

Straight ahead of him the confused inmate saw his own reflection, a half-transparent gray window stuck to the wall in a room surrounded by glass. He sat in a chair, but could see from the reflection that this chair had some sort of hood hanging over his head. Soon he realized it was an electric chair. Panicking as he tried to get loose, Timothy's glance darted futilely between the straps and the glass window. There behind the window stood a person wearing a hood.

Timothy yelled, "What are you doing? I have time! The electric chair! You—you don't use the chair anymore!"

A gruff voice from nowhere sounded back, "Of course we do!" From inside his jacket, the hooded person removed a stake-like item with wires sticking out of it as if it was meant to fasten tents to the ground. He also revealed a hammer. With conscienceless efficiency, the hooded guard entered the room and drove the stake through the inmate's skull. Lights flickered and strobed as the bolt burned downward through the rest of his body...

"Prisoner 5020!" Timothy felt a thump on the bottom of his foot which stung like hell. There was a shadow standing over him. The inmate adjusted his eyes to the prison guard. It was clear what was coming next. Without a thought Timothy sprung up to get a good hold on the guard, but froze in midair.

The guard spoke authoritatively, "Prisoner 5020 you were briefed were you not?"

The Cell

Timothy, dazed, standing, but coming back to his senses, stood still with quiet fear. "Yes Sir!" he relaxed his shaking muscles slightly as he responded.

"Well the next time you do not repeat your prisoner number you will be put in the Hole! Got it!"

"Yes sir!" Timothy answered immediately.

But his thoughts were determined to stray back to the chair and the glass room.

Timothy was, at some point, let out for exercise. While walking in a circle, 5020 thought to himself, *I can't go on like this. Afraid to sleep. What do I do? I know! I'll ask to talk to the warden to get my execution moved up.*

Back in his cell, sitting on his bunk bed, Timothy would doze off every now and then only to quickly catch himself. *Man, that was close. Let me try to think happy memories about Grandpa.* And for a while Timothy was able to smile. It worked. Not sleepy, but happy.

Suddenly there was a scraping noise. Timothy looked up. *But how could that happen? I'm sitting down. Something's swinging.* Looking all the way up, he saw it.

Some guy's body hanging from the light fixture.

A startled Timothy got the hell out of bed and rushed to the front of his cell. "Guard! Guard!" he yelled.

Dark Cloud

The guard appeared. "What the hell do you want!"

Timothy, short of breath, jerked his neck behind him over his shoulder, "Someone hung himself in my room."

The guard twisted his mouth with a skeptical "Hmph." "Turn around. Put your hands in the slot." Timothy obeyed. But as soon as Timothy turned around the body was gone. The guard handcuffed Timothy, "Now step forward." Timothy did so, but continued to wonder nervously what happened to the body.

The guard entered the cell, and looked over at Timothy's bed. "Okay where is the Hanging Man?"

"Look he was hanging over my bed!"

The guard turned to Timothy, "Get some rest. You look like you haven't slept for years."

The guard opened the cell door, and told Timothy to turn around and put his hands back to be uncuffed. "We did have a prisoner hang himself in this cell," the guard added. Then he walked off.

Timothy froze.

Having turned the corner, the guard's disguised smirk revealed itself, "Dang! I love the stories I make up." As he approached the main cellblock door he was greeted by second guard.

"What was that all about?" the second guard asked.

The Cell

"5020 said he saw someone hanging in is room. I told him he needed to get some sleep and that someone *did* hang himself. And he bought it. What a stupid motherfucker." The first guard laughed with a smirk.

The second guard appeared stern. "I wouldn't joke about that. Several prisoners have hung themselves on that cell block."

Warden

Waking up. One guard called out, "Inmate!"

Timothy, remembering the rules, shouted out "5020!" The inmate stood up, backed his way toward the cell door and put his hands in the slot to be cuffed. The guard came in, and this time shackled Timothy's legs.

"Come on let's go," the guard ordered.

They passed through several doors until they finally arrived at one not made of metal. The guard tapped on the door, to which a voice from the other side answered, "Come in!" Timothy hobbled in with the guard closely by. Before him stood the man he had met that first day he had arrived in this place, the gentleman in the suit.

"I was never properly introduced to you. I am Warden Charles MacDuff." The Warden reviewed some paperwork on his desk. "I see you have been here four months and have not caused any trouble. That's good to hear. Now since you have passed that test you will be rewarded some reading material. After you visit here, Harris—" (Timothy now realized that was his guard's name.) "—will take you to our humble library. You can read, son?"

Dark Cloud

Timothy nodded his head up and down.

"If you can't read believe me you will learn with all this time on your hands. All we have is time. Now my man do you have anything you want to share with me?"

Timothy replied, "Can you get a message to my lawyer?"

"I don't see why not!"

Timothy looked the Warden straight in the eyes and said "Tell him I want to move my execution date closer."

The Warden did not seem surprised. "The nightmares are getting to you?"

"Just tell him that for me," Timothy answered.

The Warden motioned to Harris to take the inmate away.

Contact

After passing through a darkened hallway, Timothy and Harris stopped at a door which looked like a regular cell door, except that it had no slot to put a person's hands in to be cuffed. Instead there was a small window for looking through. Harris the guard peeked through the opening. The only sight was a man with a mohawk sitting behind a desk. Harris gave an unusually formal "Psst" to get the man's attention, even though he surely could have let himself in with his own key. The mohawk man looked up, took his time rising from his desk, took his time walking over to the door, and took still more time unlocking it. With a big grin on his face, he greeted his guests.

"Hello." Mr. Mohawk acknowledged Harris, but his eyes were on Timothy. "Well who is your new friend we got here?"

Harris, keeping it professional, steered clear of the mohawk's hospitality. "This is inmate 5020."

The mysterious occupant of the room turned to Harris, "We have a man with a number for his name."

Harris gave a nod.

Timothy stared half blankly, half unsettled by Mr. Mohawk and recited his own name, "Timothy."

"What!" the man pretended either deafness or surprise. No one could say which one.

Timothy repeated his name.

"Is that so? My name is Hawk. You know why?"

Timothy wanted to say *Is it because of the hai*—

"Not because of the hair, but because I have an eye. And you are a nice-looking specimen." Turning to Harris, Hawk continued, "Isn't he Harris?"

Harris stayed stone-faced.

Hawk addressed Timothy again, "Now I am going to ask you to do something." The mohawk walked back to his desk and took out a camera. "Now I want you to untie the draw strings on your jammies there."

Timothy froze. Anyone could see what this was all about. He looked at Harris. Harris looked at him.

Just as Timothy started untying, he quickly made a move to throw an elbow at Harris. But Harris was too quick. Apparently, this had happened so often before that they were anticipating this. Harris grabbed Timothy in a lock so that he could not move his arms. Hawk efficiently and at lightning speed untied the drawstring and pulled down Timothy's pants, then his boxers. Eyeing Timothy's privates Hawk glowed with enthusiasm, "Yes! We can get something for this." He then picked up his camera and started taking pictures of Timothy's genitals.

Harris looked towards one of the walls as if he had better things to do, "Do you want to do the money shot?"

Hawk replied, "Not now. Let's see what our clients will pay for this. Who knows? They might want more." He then pulled up Timothy's boxers and pants. "Okay, now let's read some library books."

Timothy stood petrified over what had just taken place.

"Harris I think you can let him go now." The guard loosened his grip on Timothy. "Okay! It seems like the cat's got your tongue. I'll pick a book out for you." Hawk then vanished behind some shelves and came back with two books.

"Okay what about these two?" Hawk showed the first one to Timothy and then the second one. They seemed almost identical. "So what do you think?"

Timothy responded lifelessly, "Indians."

Hawks face instantly boiled in a furious red. "They are NATIVE AMERICANS you fucking—"

Timothy was just waiting for Hawk to break out the N word, then it would have been all over. But Hawk caught himself. Harris eyed Hawk carefully. With renewed restraint, Hawk continued calmly, "*Huff* Native Americans. They are *Native* Americans."

Timothy repeated, "Native Americans." *Just to calm this psycho down*, he thought to himself.

Harris looked at his watch. "Alright time's up boys."

As Harris and Timothy turned to exit, Hawk called out to Timothy. "Oh yes, almost forgot! Here is some peanut butter. This is my welcoming package to you."

Harris grabbed the plastic baggy and escorted Timothy out.

Back in his cell, Timothy sat confused and ashamed. *What the fuck? Some psycho takes pictures of my dick...Native Indians...peanut butter.* After looking around some more at different corners of the cell walls, he finally decided to open one of the books in hopes of easing his mind. Crazy as they were, the thoughts that occupied him now weren't the problem. It was the dreams. Especially the dreams.

As Timothy flipped through the pages he eventually took interest in an Indian named Geronimo, Apache Chief. Barely staying awake, Timothy really wanted to read more. But in a little more than an hour, sleep finally took over. And so did the dreams.

Timothy shook himself awake just in time for the cell guard to call his number, which he immediately repeated. A seed had been planted, though. Later during exercise Timothy would realize that he could not wait to get back to his book.

The inmate felt a connection to this person Geronimo. With his thoughts imbedded in the book, he noticed the beautiful artwork, the American Natives' clothing, the scenery. At one point he picked up a pencil and started looking around for some paper. In the back of the book there was a blank sheet. Figuring that psycho Hawk probably wouldn't notice a minor change in the prison's property, he tore out the blank page and started drawing on it.

Inspecting what he had just drawn, Timothy was filled with excitement. He also found himself hungry. It was getting late though, so he decided to grab some crackers he had saved for a rainy day. With the peanut butter added on top, he started munching. Sitting calmly for the first time in a long while, Timothy proudly tilted his drawing at different angles as he snacked on his victory meal. Fatigue came sooner than expected after long hours of drawing, so he decided to call it a night.

Another bad dream. This one featured nauseating images of guts everywhere. On the walls, soaked in the sheets, and all over the floor. Waking up in the middle of the night, Timothy's stomach coiled and heaved in a dizzying pain. He hunched over in a near crawl as he reached to turn on the light, only to realize that he had vomit and shit all over himself. Splattered in a mess of his own, he stumbled as he tried to call to the guard. A half-word came out along with more vomit. Even more shit poured into his pants. No way to stop any of it. The inmate spread his palms to the slimy floor and fell over.

Timothy opened his eyes, blinking in the blinding brightness of the room. Closing his eyes proved easier. Finally a man with a lab coat appeared over him.

"Well, well. Welcome back," began a dry yet unexcitable voice, probably a doctor's. And this place was probably a hospital. "I see the IV fluids are working. When they brought you in here you were quite dehydrated. Let's just say you had food poisoning. And we found this in your room."

The doctor held up the empty plastic baggy.

"We tested this, and it seems you received some sort of ¿special brew? of peanut butter. Do you know what this is?"

Timothy shook his head sideways.

The doctor filled in the blanks. "Well what some people have been known to do is quite nasty. It's just like cocaine. You know they add more substance to make it stretch so they can sell it in higher quantities."

But Timothy had dealt drugs. He knew what he had eaten was definitely not cocaine or peanut butter. Or maybe it *was* peanut butter…with God knows what else in it—

"But in this case, they seem to have added…" The doctor looked at his chart. "It says '*human fecal matter*' to make it stretch.

Yes sir, you received food poisoning via someone's waste or 'shit' if you will."

Timothy lie there dumb with disbelief, but his head still spun from the illness that had gripped him hours (or maybe days?) earlier. All he could think of was getting his hands on that little shit, Hawk.

The doctor went on, "I am going to give you a pill to take to clear this up. But do me a favor. Beware of what people give you around here."

Timothy lay back in his cell, still weak. He heard one of the guards coming with his food, along with his pill to take. Harris appeared for a brief moment, looked at Timothy, shook his head and walked off. The floor still stank.

Timothy remained almost catatonic in his cell. The book didn't interest him anymore. Just Hawk. Finally the guard called out, "Inmate!"

Timothy managed a loud but hoarse "5020!" It was the same routine. Timothy stepped back and held the position. The guard Harris said nothing to Timothy about where they were going, but took the books from the cell and gave them to another guard.

Dark Cloud

While approaching the library, Harris pulled Timothy from the back toward him and whispered, "I know how you feel but don't do anything stupid!" Then they proceeded.

Harris opened the door to the library, and there sat Hawk looking pleasantly surprised "Hey! There he i—"

Before Hawk could finish his greeting, Timothy spit in his face. Hawk's glasses dripped with the aftermath.

Harris reacted quickly, "I told you!" he grit his teeth, and jammed Timothy in the side with his club. The impact was so hard Timothy's knees buckled like a windblown card house. The inmate would have sank to the floor had the guard not used an extra stern vice grip forcing him to keep standing.

Hawk pulled a napkin from his desk and wiped his face and glasses. "Well happy to see you too!" Suddenly Hawk "realized" something. "Shit! I gave you the wrong batch! Seems like you are doing okay, though!"

Timothy was angrier than ever. "Okay!? If I had—"

Harris yanked the inmate hard by the handcuffs. Timothy was easily restrained.

Hawk proceeded, "Okay, let's get down to business. They need money shots. They like what they saw but does it work?"

Man, what the f—!? Timothy reeled back at Hawk's bald audacity.

Contact

The mohawk continued Timothy's briefing. "Remember last time? Well this time you need to… let's just say…make a deposit. Would you like me to do the honor or can we trust you if Hank uncuffed you?"

What!? (No time for revenge at all.) Having been at this place for long enough, Timothy had long forgotten how to think up anything different from what he was told. It wasn't a question of *if* he would do it, but how, and how quickly he could answer. *No man is gonna touch me. If he does, it's on.* So Timothy gave in, choosing to fulfill the perverse request himself.

Hawk retrieved his camera while Harris uncuffed him. Timothy turned off his thoughts, reached down his pants and closed his eyes. His girlfriend was his only focus. In no time he heard Hawk, "This is the money shot!"

Several clicks later it was all over.

Hawk gave Timothy a towel, along with some smirking advice. "You know in order to buy good peanut butter—or any other items—around this place, you need to have money on the books. Like a bank account." Hawk showed Timothy a pink piece of paper that had $10.00 printed on it like monopoly money. "I guess this is your first time seeing prison money. Well get used to it. This is your cut from the last picture." Then he slipped the phony bill into Timothy's waste band.

Dark Cloud

Harris handed the two books to Hawk, where they were briefly inspected. "I do hope you enjoyed these. Did you want to stay with Native Americans?"

Timothy lowered his head. *Powerless… Some pervert's bitch on death row.* "Sure, American. Native." Hawk disappeared in the back just like the previous time, and came out with three more books. Timothy saw the extra book and tried to console himself. *Maybe this motherfucker felt guilty.* Then the inmate chuckled a little inside, *We're all guilty.*

Hawk handed the books to Harris, "Enjoy, 5020!"

Just after Harris escorted Timothy out, Hawk began putting up the books. One of the books dropped, and as it fell to the floor a sheet of paper floated out. Hawk picked up the sheet and frowned, realizing it was torn from the book. "That fucker!" But it wasn't the ripped page that drew Hawk's attention. It was the inmate's drawing of a Native American.

Back in his cell, Timothy took the $10 pink slip out of his pocket. Humiliating. But it beat getting raped. Timothy thought about the idea of getting money on the books, and gradually turned his attention to what other kinds of things he could get from outside his cell. It wasn't freedom, but it was probably as close to freedom as he would ever get from here on. *Things from the outside…I need more information.*

While sitting on his bed, Timothy opened one of the items he had checked out. Suddenly he remembered the drawing. *Shit! I left it in the book!* Now wondering if Hawk had found the torn page, Timothy grew nervous. Then he tried to convince himself it was no big deal. *So what, I fucked up one of his books. Fucking pervert!* The inmate began reading, and again ripped out a sheet from the back of the book. He started drawing, but this time he would remember not to leave it in the book.

Over time Timothy realized his bad dreams were disappearing, as he began regularly roaming the land like his Native American friends.

Payment

Just as one of the guards exited Hawk's library with his inmate in tow, Hawk heard the door slam. The mohawk had been so absorbed in thought regarding 5020's drawing a few weeks earlier, that he hadn't paid much attention to the man who had just entered wearing an inmate's uniform. The slight sound of heavy breathing, however, did get Hawk's attention.

"Ah, 4804 can I help you?" Hawk greeted the man. Upon second look, he noticed a fork in the inmate's hand. Except it was missing the ends. Suddenly Hawk's usual smirk turned dead serious. That was no fork. It was a shank.

The inmate seemed almost deranged with desperation. "Man where'z my money you promise me?"

Hawk calculated that stalling would be his best bet, giving him a chance to dash to the door. "I told you 4804. It'll be two weeks. It's not two weeks yet." Hawk sounded as nonchalant as ever.

The inmate's voice shook, "I need it now or they're gonna kill me!"

Hawk turned his head to the side with a shrug, "Hey give me till tomorrow and I should have it."

Dark Cloud

"No! Now! You have me do these sick things, I need money now!" The angry inmate began his advance.

So much for stalling. Hawk tried to create a diversion by throwing the book he was holding at the inmate and making a run for the door. But the inmate speedily ducked the book and knocked it aside, grabbing Hawk by the hair as he tried to pass. Hair in the left hand and a shank in the right, the inmate let out a mad roar as he dug the weapon into the easiest spot on Hawk's face he could find. Hawk elbowed his assailant in the chest and kicked him in shin, knocking the attacker back a little and loosening the hold on his hair. The hand had a mind of its own as the door was thrown open, Hawk running out of the library screaming with the shank protruding from his eye. Less than ten seconds later, armed guards had tackled the shocked and bloodied Hawk as well as the raging inmate who was still throwing books around with an ear-splitting "Fuck! FUUUCK! Fuck!!" back in the library.

Pictures

Three months had passed since Timothy had last visited the library. Drawing on anything he could get his hands-on, Timothy had begun getting followers—guards usually—who were impressed. Some even brought him paper in exchange for a picture.

Things had been going fairly smoothly until the day Timothy received a certain phone call. It was his lawyer. "Mr. Thomas, I did receive your request to uh, speed up your execution." But Timothy, now in prison for two (going on three) years had forgotten all about that wish.

His lawyer continued, "This request is odd but we did move forward and it *is* being processed."

Timothy held the phone with a frightened look on his face. He shuddered as he answered, "I, I, I *changed my mind*!"

The lawyer paused for a second, with a sigh that could barely be heard, "Sorry son, but you should have considered what you were really asking for. We can't just undo these things. I'm sorry."

Timothy pleaded, "This was all new. The dreams wouldn't stop! But they have now!" He yelled into the phone, with tears quickly filling up his eyes, "I don't want to die!"

The guard nearby hastily snatched the phone from Timothy's hand, then escorted him back to his cell.

Timothy shook his head low, "What did I do?" He couldn't stop hyperventilating. "What did I do?"

After a long and sleepless night, Timothy was escorted the next morning down a familiar hallway to the library. A new guard had taken over the duties, while Harris the old guard had disappeared. The library door dragged open, and behind the desk sat a transformed Hawk. The scandalous librarian now wore a full head of hair and an eye patch.

Hawk looked up with a familiar smirk on his face, "Well hello my friend! Long time no see!"

Timothy had become more talkative by now. And once again shocked by Hawk, the inmate was perplexed enough to forget about the hard night before. "What happened to your eye?"

Hawk smiled strangely, "It's a long story." The former mohawk continued to stare at Timothy. "So, word around here is all about your paintings of Native Americans. I also heard you were exchanging them for supplies?"

Timothy nodded his head.

Pictures

"What if I could make you some money?"

But Timothy was still suspicious of Hawk, wondering what had happened to his porn business. *I bet it's connected to why he has that patch.* In response to Hawk's question, Timothy had a request instead. "That sounds good but one thing I'd appreciate is if you could help me send one of my paintings to my grandparents."

Hawk was cooperative. "Let me see what I can do." Going back to his bookshelf he retrieved three books, showing them to Timothy before handing them to the guard.

Timothy commented, "I forgot about the books I checked out months ago."

Hawk looked at Timothy with an uncharacteristically puzzled face. "What books?"

Timothy replied, "Nevermind."

Back in his cell, Timothy spent some time carefully arranging his books on the table. As he was doing this, an envelope fell out. Timothy picked up the envelope and opened it. Inside he found five prison $10 pink slips, along with a note. "My porn business was shut down." The short little message made Timothy wonder even more about what happened to Harris, his prison guard.

Dark Cloud

As months went by, then years, Timothy successfully made a name for himself in the prison. Some called him "The Warrior" because of his love of creating Native American Indian paintings. He did try his hand at woodcarving, and even made some very nice furniture, but preferred painting more than anything else. He knew the end was coming soon, and that his work would also end. But maybe the best part of him would still live on through his paintings.

Timothy was escorted by the prison guards into a room that had only two chairs and a table. His lawyer came in, whom Timothy had not seen since the sentencing. Their communication after that had been by phone only, never in person. The lawyer greeted him. "Hello, Mr. Thomas. I guess you know why I am here."

Timothy nodded.

"I am trying my best to have people write letters on your behalf, and I've been appealing." The lawyer paused and waited for a response, but his client was clearly tired. "Do you have anything to say?"

Timothy initially sat there speechless as he learned the details of his coming execution. The end was now very near, only two weeks away. After two or three seconds of blank but hardened staring right through his lawyer, the inmate finally answered. "Just tell my grandparents I'm sorry."

Pictures

After his lawyer left, Timothy was escorted back to his cell. He took out the biggest canvas he had left, stopped to write a request to Hawk, and then started painting.

Procedures

A guard was in Warden MacDuff's office while the head of the prison was going through paperwork. One of the files stood out, prompting the guard to call the Warden's attention.

"Sir this execution is scheduled for next week."

The Warden looked at the name on the file, then at one particular painting on his office wall. He then commented, "Have you noticed this inmate never signs his work? Being black and all, he hasn't turned into a Muslim either. Rather, he belongs to an Indian tribe."

The guard replied, "I don't know much about that, sir."

"Well let's make sure we have everything set up for this execution next week, the usual hole dug. I doubt that the family wants the body. They never do. Tags, tombstone, etc."

Hawk

Timothy was taken to the library for the very last time. Hawk started off with his back turned to the inmate, but as soon as Hawk turned around his face was painted. Timothy, startled again, recognized the markings as war paint.

Hawk chimed, "I thought this was the least I could do to honor you."

If Timothy had been frowning when he entered the library, now he frowned slightly less. "Do you have a book elaborating on Huntsville and the prison system?"

Hawk was sarcastically curious, "*Why?*"

"I just need to read up on some things about this place," the inmate explained.

"You don't know enough right now? Man, they are going to kill you!" Hawk puzzled out loud.

Hearing this sent chills through Timothy's body more real than any imagined execution chemicals. Hawk disappeared in the back and came out with a book in hand. Timothy sampled the book and then made his final request to Hawk.

Dark Cloud

"I am gonna have a painting delivered to you and it's a must that my grandparents get it."

"Okay Bro."

Timothy turned around and left, while Hawk stood there.

The Delivery

Outside the Imagine Art Studio in Santa Fe, New Mexico, a FedEx truck pulled up in front. The driver entered the art studio with a package in hand. Sitting behind a desk in the reception area was a well-dressed gentleman. The man looked up suddenly with a big smile when the bells on the door rang. His smile grew even bigger when he saw the package.

"Hello, Pete! How is everything going for you today?"

Pete the deliveryman responded, "Same as always, Roger! I would love to take a look at this painting but I have to run. It's larger than the others you've gotten from this particular address over the years."

Roger took the package from Pete.

"Oh yes, I almost forgot to give you this. It was attached to it. I didn't want it to fall off." Pete handed the small envelope to Roger. "Well, got to run. See ya!"

Roger nodded. His main interest was what was in the package.

Roger carried the package through the main showroom which was full of paintings, particularly Native American works. Arriving at the back of the store, he knocked on the door. A voice at the other side answered, "Come in!" And Roger entered with his usual big smile.

"We got another delivery. This one is larger than all the others."

Behind the desk sat a beautiful woman in retro dress. As she turned her eyes to the package, her excitement instantly began to build. She told Roger, "Well what are you waiting for? Unwrap it!"

Roger unwrapped the package, and observed for the painting for a while in astonishment. Suddenly, however, his surprise turned blank as he looked up at the lady, then at the painting again.

"What's wrong?" she asked him.

Roger handed the painting to her.

"It's beautiful," she noted. Then she looked closely.

Roger asked cautiously, "Do you see what I see?" Then he handed her the envelope. "This came with it."

The lady opened the letter and read it. "Roger, what date is on the package?"

Roger sifted through the wrapping. "It says March 30."

"Uh! This was in the mail for a month! Shit!" She set the painting down and rushed out. Left there lying on the desk, the painting's image was clearly a portrait of her.

The Delivery

The lady passed through the main showroom, several of whose paintings were in a style similar to the one she had just gotten. A few of those paintings had sold signs on them with price tags ranging from $1,000 to $3,000.

Back in the office, Roger noticed a signature.

The Meal

The priest stood inside the cell, "Let us Pray."

With his hand on top of Timothy's head, he recited the rites. "Bless this young man as he embarks on another journey in life. Bless you my child, and may you go in peace." Scattered around the room were a half-eaten burger and fries, a carton of chocolate milk, and a couple of used ketchup packets. These were what Timothy had requested for his last meal, a memory of what was always on the menu back in school every Thursday. Timothy looked down at his hands. They were trembling, palms sweating. Then he closed his eyes. The screams repeated from some distant place inside his head, "I don't want to die."

The guards were now outside his cell.

The Execution

The group proceeded down the hallway, one armed guard in front, followed by the priest, then Timothy hobbling with shackles on his ankles, handcuffs on his wrists. Two more guards walked along each side of the prisoner, and another one close behind. They eventually came to the execution chamber, where a gurney sat in the middle of the room.

The guards maneuvered Timothy to the gurney, and without any hesitation instructed the prisoner to sit. The guards initiated Timothy's movements. Slowly, but forcefully they positioned Timothy on the gurney, stopped his legs from swinging slightly, unshackled him and strapped the legs apart. As the guards took off the prisoner's handcuffs, Timothy thought for once how he wished they would leave them on. The right arm was strapped, then the left, followed by him being strapped around the waist.

Timothy looked straight ahead at the room's glass window, wondering if there were any people on the other side. He wondered if grandma and grandpa were there. In past executions they would place a hood over the head, but in this case death would not be as gruesome as the electric chair, better known as "Old Sparky." It wasn't as gruesome, but it was still unimaginably frightening no matter how it took place. The inmate became overwhelmed; his body started to shake.

Timothy began to panic. Some voice said, "Relax. If you don't, you are just going to make it very unpleasant for yourself." There in the room stood the person who was going to administer the lethal injections. On the other side was a room no larger than a closet with a man behind the door and a window large enough to watch the prisoner's every move.

In this case, the man behind the door was waiting for the Governor's response to see if Timothy's life would be spared. He looked at his watch 1 minute before midnight. The phone rang. The gentleman picked up quickly. The person who was about to begin the procedure suddenly stopped, turning to watch the man who had just picked up the phone in the small room. The person administering and the man on the phone made eye contact. Shortly thereafter, the man on the phone shook his head up and down. Administering of the injections would begin now.

As the executioner picked up the first of three syringes for administering, Timothy started to struggle in the gurney. The executioner signaled for the guard to get a tighter grip on the prisoner. The needle penetrated Timothy's arm through the vein, causing a bubble to form which quickly swelled to the size of a golf ball. The needle was removed, then drilled into another vein. Its fluid, Sodium Thiopental, flowed slowly out of the syringe, beginning its work in rendering the offender unconscious. Timothy started to relax. Unable to move, he was soon fully paralyzed. The second syringe, Pancuronium

The Delivery

Bromide, would cause further paralysis and collapse the lungs. With his eyes blinking out of control, Timothy stared helplessly at nothing specific. Flashes of his childhood, Grandma, Pa Pa, and in his room on the nightstand a birthday card reading "Happy Birthday, Timothy!" from Daniel, the kid he had killed. A handgun rested on top of the card. A third syringe, Potassium Chloride, was injected to stop the heart. And so it did, with a loud gunshot. It was the last thing Timothy heard in his brain. The doctor came in and felt Timothy's carotid pulse. He looked up at the man in the window and nodded his head up and down, confirmation that the prisoner had passed.

Outside the steps of the Walls Unit, Timothy Walt Thomas' death was announced.

The Arrival

She arrived at the airport and rushed to hail a cab. "I need to go to Huntsville State Prison."

The cab driver looked at her and was intrigued. He wondered why such a beautiful woman would want to go to an awful place like that.

She glared back at him, "What the hell are you looking at me like that for?"

They drove off.

"Never been to Huntsville before?" The cab driver sensed that the lady wanted to go to the Walls Unit where the executions took place.

As they pulled up to the front, the lady quickly exited the cab, forgetting that she had to pay. The cab driver asked, "Miss do you want me to stay?"

"No!" she snapped at him. Then she headed towards the entrance, where a guard immediately stopped her in her tracks.

"What is your purpose here?"

"To see a friend," she replied.

"Sorry but this not where we house regular prisoners. Plus if they are just a friend, there are procedures."

"It's my son." The lady thought back to the last time she had seen Timothy. In the courtroom on the day he got sentenced, she was the first person to leave after the verdict.

"Still ma'am for regular visits—" Seeing the urgency and frustration in her eyes, however, the guard stopped. He knew. "I will escort you to the front desk."

Once they made it to the front desk, the guard told the clerk that the visitor was looking for her son. The clerk waited for her to provide more details.

"Timothy Thomas," she said.

"I need a full name."

"Timothy Walt Thomas." The guard remained behind her.

"You will find Mr. Timothy Walt Thomas at this address, and here is his number."

With some relief, the lady thanked the clerk and was escorted out. While exiting she thought, *Does Timothy have more paintings for my shop to survive?* Over the years she had made over a million dollars living the life.

The Arrival

Two years after Timothy had been sentenced to death, she had visited her parents. There in the living room were five packages. She had asked her parents about them. They told her the paintings were going to be burned. She had examined one of the packages and seen the return address in Huntsville. Upon unwrapping the package she discovered a work of Native American art. Finding there was no signature, her eyes lit up. She immediately told her parents that she would take the packages off their hands, and later went to the post office to fill out a card diverting anything from Huntsville to her home address in New Mexico.

But now she urgently needed to talk to him. The guard offered on their way out, "Would you like for me to call you a cab?" But before she could answer him, there was the cab that brought her to the prison. She dashed to the cab and handed him the address she had gotten.

"Take me to this address ASAP!"

The cab driver took the piece of paper and glanced at it as he pulled out. Then he handed the address back to her saying, "I think you are going to need this. Ma'am are you sure you want to go there now? It's starting to get dark."

Through the rear-view mirror they made eye contact. She shouted, "Take me to that damned address NOW!"

Dark Cloud

The drive only took five minutes. Upon arrival, the cab driver slowed down. The lady was talking on the phone.

"Yes, yes, good news. I am on my way to see him now." The voice on the other end noted that *The painting is different*. She got out of the cab and paid, and the driver immediately left.

Still on the phone, the lady responded, "How is the picture different? I know it's the largest one we ever received…"

The voice on the other end, Roger noted, "It's signed."

"It's signed!?" The lady finally looked up at where she was. The sign read "Joe Byrd Cemetery." She panicked out loud, "What the fuck?"

"What's going on?" Roger had to know.

"I think someone is playing a joke. Do me a favor look up this address." She gave Roger the address before continuing. "You'd better call me back. My cell phone is about to die."

"Ok."

The lady stood there thinking there might be a building farther back. So she decided to go in. Looking up, she saw that darkness would surely be coming soon.

In no time she began to see headstones. One row, then another. Then the headstones turned to crosses. Walking straight ahead, she noticed the incline was going uphill. *Maybe a building will be over this hill.* Meanwhile, she started seeing some of the engravings on the crosses. A few could be read, but

The Arrival

some were so old that nothing but stone remained. Finally she reached the top of the hill, only to lose all breath in a gasp at what she saw. Nothing but crosses.

My God.

Then it came to her. The address on the piece of paper the clerk had written down. "No! No!" the lady panicked as she started shaking all over. She left that hill, trying to find an exit, but instead stumbled over two fresh graves.

Her phone rang, startling her. Roger delivered the news, "You are not going to believe this. The address is Joe Byrd Cemetery, this is where they bury the prisoners after they are executed and the bodies aren't claimed by family members." While Roger continued talking, the lady leaned over and looked at a nameplate on one of the graves. Knowing her phone was about to die, she used the light to reveal the name. Timothy Walt Thomas, with a code number. She took another look at the paper with the address, trying to make sense of what she was seeing.

Roger finally got to this point as the signal cut out then cut back in, "…they exe..uted him!"

The lady stood and backed up in disbelief. The signal was now lost for good, and seconds later, all power to the phone.

Roger eventually hung up and tried calling again, but the call went straight to her voice mail. Suddenly he remembered something that had been bothering him. He inspected the

Dark Cloud

bottom of the painting again. It wasn't a signature, but a code number that must have been very important.

The cab driver drove his cab back to the station and parked his cab. He stood by his car for a little while, then got back in. He put on his hat, lit up a cigar, and slowly pulled out of the parking lot.

The cab passed by a few noteworthy places. The Walls Unit, Sam Houston State University, Sam Houston Cemetery, Joe Byrd Cemetery.

Somewhere in Santa Fe, New Mexico stands Imagine Art, a For Sale sign on the door.

A native San Antonian and founder of The Vintage Club Stories, Writer/Producer, Cynthia Bergen has been active in film and film societies since 2009. She began by writing short stories which received notice from her professors at St. Phillips College. Her professors in turn encouraged her to move forward. Shortly after finishing her education, Cynthia self-published her first book of short stories based on true life events, *Vintage Club Stories Volume I*. Soon after, her work received the attention of local directors, leading to her entry into short film. Award winning Writer/Director Issac Rodriquez joined forces with Cynthia in 2014, where the two established "No Sleep Films." Working with Isaac, Cynthia has produced multiple award winning short films and feature films which have, to date, been screened in over 300 film festivals all over the world. Several have gone viral. Follow Cynthia at

www.facebook.com/nosleepchannel
www.youtube/c/nosleep1
vintageclubstories.com